The Weight of the Shadows

Patricia Terry

Red Dust . New York

Tropical Architecture first appeared in The Hudson Review.
Different versions of Two Deerhounds, Hawk, Barn Owls were
published in ArtWord Quarterly.
My thanks to the editors of these publications.

The following poems which appear in this book are excerpts from larger
poems:
Fragments of Winter
Two Deerhounds
Rainhawk
Barn Owls
Neighboring Trees, Clouds and Mountains
Patagonia
Afterword

Design lay-out by Alexander Gray and Joanna Gunderson

The Weight of the Shadows by Patricia Terry
copyright ©2001 Patricia Terry
Published by Red Dust, Inc.

ISBN 0-87376-090

Fragments of Winter

Hard to believe
that it isn't the weight of the shadows,
the long flexible shadows of stiff perpendiculars, trees,
that carved these undulations
into the snowfield

A long weed with a pointed beak
dips under the rain into
a puddle in the snow
like a thin crane searching
and searching again.

There is nothing else alive here
except for me.

In the space framed by the window:
pliable branches, leafless,
and hemlock fronds
with the wind
prowling among them, touching them
here and there, alighting,
releasing its weight, alighting
and moving on

Close to twilight
the low ranges of hills
were as never before,
every row a different kind of grey,
and, after the foreground mist
drifting, blurring the snow,
each one distinct from the next
until the ultimate line was almost black,
of such a clarity
there could be nothing beyond it but the sky.

Because of the papery husks
of beech leaves,
no breeze comes into the woods
quite silently.

By the time of the first crocuses,
pale tan against clear grey has come to seem
more than adequate color.

Natural Things

Tropical Architecture

What seems to have been lacking
when I first admired the palm trees,
the Royal Palms,
was remembering how certain Egyptian columns
swell out like slender ladies
neatly wrapped down to the feet,
to a mathematical elegance of line
found, more often than not,
in natural things
like those horizontally banded trees
rising grey-brown straight
toward parenthetical curves
and a bright green Modigliani neck
above which unwieldy coiffures
click and interlace in the breeze.

Horse and Rider

for Simone Koster

Vertical immobility
and horizontal momentum
are aligned.

The cause of the movement
no longer impedes it.

A change of tempo
in the mind
will alter the cadence.
A change of cadence
alters the rhythm
of the mind.

There is one
attention

giving a form to space.

Two Deerhounds

as smooth among the trees
as their shadows;

they feel the reach of their legs
the stone walls going by
below them, not dogs running only
the trees giving way.

Rainhawk

The rain looked like ruled lines that gleamed
straight down and along one heavier vertical
the hawk on top of it
as quiet as wood

Hawk

I waited for him like a hunter.
I willed him to light.
The wind ruffled his feathers, soft underneath like fur.
His beak slicked his back.
He cried, "Mine! Mine! Mine!"
Tawny-bronze ruff, Persian patterns over his body

Austere as an axe of jade.

He shifted his grip
His eyes locked into mine,
Then the up-surge in his shoulders,
His weight the weight of the air that breathes as he glides.

Barn Owls

fly silent as smoke
and the evening
gathers around them
enclosing the last of the light,
a triangular pallor, a face,
surrounding black holes that are eyes

Snow Geese

From the last opaque hollows under dawn,
the high-pitched wavering sound
of snow geese,
a dome of vibrations
over the frozen lake
and over us as we wait
to see what will happen
when the white multitude stirs.
Can we withstand
so much of anything?
We ourselves might let go
take off on a steep slope upwards
when a thunder of drumming feathers loosens the
	ground
which rises, all at once, a second sky
reaching toward us
the gloss of beaks crying out
black wingtips marking the tempo
horizon to horizon
an avalanche of undulating brightness

And then a linear glitter
almost out of sight.

Neighboring Trees, Clouds and Mountains

for Robert

They grew up side by side,
gradually attracting all the water,
and now they stand alone,
each of them reaching out
its longest fronds to the other's.
Their leaves glitter like metal.

They look, from their great distance, into our house,
neither menacing nor protective,
but with somber intensity.

It isn't long before you notice the clouds.
They bloom like a ceremony behind the backs of the
         hills, wisps, tendrils
plumes expanding
to brilliantly illuminated
convoluted mounds, grey pearl over white
with a glow of fire inside,
violent in shape, an avalanche cresting
                              colossal
    explosions
              too heavy
      to stay up
                        but you never see them

disappear
       and they do,
every time.

The sun here is invisible most of the time
blurred by its own brilliance
but late in the day
a globe
larger than a harvest moon
the color of red embers,
clear or cloud-streaked, sharp-edged,
moves toward the horizon, pulled
evenly downward so fast
you can scarcely take a breath
before it is gone.

It's hard to tell about the mountains.
They move all the time - one morning
they were only a drift of volcanic islands
on silvery emptiness.
There seems no end of them.
You don't see the same one twice.

Toward evening they extend from their remoteness
a veil over the landscape
all blue and shadowed blue,
simplified, unfurrowed.

Once in a while,
at the very farthest point to the right
where the mountains really do come to an end
there seems to be a rectangle of light,
and that is the sea.

Patagonia

for Kathleen Micklow

Peninsula Valdès

At the day's end
the light receded not toward a horizon
but into what appeared a sea beyond
the edge of the land, a clear flameless
burning
interrupted here and there by islands,
clouds.

Punta Tumbo Penguins

Their multitudes,
enough to darken the hills, in conversation
make the noise of innumerable bees.

On the Plateau

Here is where the wind blows under heaven
having swept the whole earth bare
even of dust.
One wind following another.

     The pine tree
          a sharp-nosed shadow puppet
               determined to walk forward.

A white-green lake
hisses, twisting upward,
more air than water.

          On a hillside the wind
          breathes in my place
          nothing
          only the strength
          to stay there.

Toward Tierra del Fuego

The clouds are wrapping themselves around the
mountains rising higher and higher

        iron mountains
        indented like leaves.

The clenched fist of that peak
must have been pried open
by vague fingers of water now
a core of ice, bright blue against the stone.

Afterword

The tall bending grass on the hillside
suddenly straightens, remains
for moments each stalk perpendicular,
then
a sheet of reflected light